# BRITISH INFANTRY REGIMENTS

## 1660-1914

by A. H. Bowling

ALMARK  PUBLISHING  CO.,  LONDON

First Published—August 1970

ISBN  85524  000  8  (hard  cover  edition)
ISBN  85524  001  6  (paper  covered  edition)

*By the same author:*
*SCOTTISH REGIMENTS, 1660-1914*

Printed in Great Britain by
Vale Press Ltd., Mitcham, Surrey,
for the publishers, Almark Publishing Co.
104-106 Watling Avenue, Edgware,
Middlesex, England.

# Introduction

THIS book is a companion volume to *Scottish Regiments 1660-1914* and it is intended that the two publications between them should give a concise, but comprehensive, coverage of the history of the British infantry regiments and their uniforms in the period up to 1914, after which the widespread wearing of full-dress uniforms was largely discontinued. The Scottish regiments were given separate treatment, for their histories and uniforms varied considerably from other British Army infantry regiments. In this present book, the subject of British infantry is given the more extensive treatment that the generally standardised nature of the uniform allows. Highland dress is, in fact, illustrated but there is no duplication of what has already appeared in *Scottish Regiments*. Apart from the 114 colour drawings which show the development of British infantry uniforms from 1660-1914, there are groups of multi-view line drawings which show the major uniform changes for each main period of British military history. These drawings, showing the figure from various aspects, are intended particularly to assist model soldier enthusiasts.

In addition to the uniform details, there is a double page of weapon drawings depicting to scale (where possible) the changing side arms of the British infantryman over the 1660-1914 period. Weapons peculiar to Scottish regiments, are, however, omitted since these are included in the companion volume. Full details of title and regimental changes are given, but for convenience the 1914 title is frequently used to avoid complicated cross-referencing; this is indicated at the appropriate points in the text, however. Photographic coverage is as thorough as space allows, though it will be appreciated that actual pictures can only date from the latter half of the nineteenth century. All the pictures are from the author's personal collection and have been chosen judiciously with a view to both showing essential detail and to conveying the 'atmosphere' of British infantryman in Victorian times. Many of these pictures are hitherto unpublished. There are also a number of contemporary prints, not so reliable as photographs, but nonetheless of great interest.

## CONTENTS

ABOVE: Brigade of Guards, 1866. The first figure shows the undress tunic
worn by a Staff Sergeant, Coldstream Guards. This is scarlet with
plain blue collar and cuffs piped white. The forage cap is dark blue with
a band of gold lace and gold trimming on the peak. His sword scabbard
is black with brass fittings. Next, is the Regimental Sergeant Major,
Scots Guards, wearing the Warrant Officers' tunic with gold lace on the
collar and cuffs. The badge of rank worn on both arms, is the Royal
Arms superimposed on a gold 4 bar chevron. The soldier in a grey
greatcoat is a private of the Coldstream Guards. His red plume is on
the right of the bearskin. The pioneer of the Grenadier Guards wears
the white crossed axes and grenades on both arms. FRONT COVER:
Colour Sergeant, Grenadier Guards, 1866. There were three grades of
tunic in the Guards for ranks below that of officer; they were Warrant
Officer, Sergeant, and Other Ranks. The sergeants were distinguished
by gold lace on the cuffs. The colour badge was worn on both arms, and
the crimson sash was worn over the right shoulder.

# Part 1: 1660-1800

THE beginnings of the British Army in the form of a regular force came on the accession of Charles II. The first regiments to be embodied were the ones that had served either as Parliamentary forces or, as in the case of the Grenadier Guards, as a regiment that had served King Charles in exile. The earliest regiments to join the 'standing' Army were the regiments later to be known as The Life Guards, The Royal Horse Guards, The Grenadier Guards and The Coldstream Guards to be followed a few years later by the regiments which eventually became The Royal Scots, The Queen's and The Buffs. Gradually more regiments were added, especially between the years 1685 to 1701. These regiments saw much service on the Continent, serving in France, Belgium and Holland between 1692 and 1711. Those regiments serving with the Duke of Marlborough's forces added many famous battle honours to their historical records, and the engagements concerned included Blenheim, Ramilles, Oudenarde and Malplaquet.

The War of the Austrian Succession was especially of note, as the Battle of Dettingen in 1743 was the last conflict in which British troops were commanded in the field by the reigning king. From now on the British Army was constantly on service throughout the world and major engagements included the Capture of Quebec in 1759, the North American campaign of 1763-4, and much service in India including the Battle of Plassey in 1757. The Seven Years War, 1756-1763, resulted in one of the greatest of all actions for the British infantry. This was the Battle of Minden in which six regiments supported by Hannoverian and Hessian troops routed a French army estimated at 50,000 men. The six regiments concerned, later to become the Suffolks, Lancashire Fusiliers, Royal Welsh Fusilier, King's Own Scottish Borderers, Royal Hampshire, and King's Own Yorkshire Light Infantry, still celebrate Minden Day.

The American War of Independence, 1775-1782, saw very many British infantry regiments engaged and a great number of lessons were learnt during this period especially with regard to the use of light infantry and the adaptation of clothing to suit the conditions of a new type of warfare. The Seige of Gibraltar, 1779 to 1783, was another important episode in the history of the British infantry. Here only five regiments, later to become the Suffolks, Dorsetshires, Essex, Northamptonshire, and Highland Light Infantry, supported by contingents of the Royal Artillery and the Royal Sappers and Miners, withstood a seige by Spanish and French forces. All the infantry regiments concerned were granted the motto 'Montis Insignia Calpe' to be borne on the colours and were granted the badge of a Castle and Key, part of the arms of Gibraltar.

## UNIFORMS 1660 TO 1800

Throughout the period of full dress uniforms the British infantry was always mainly distinguished by the red coat, though there were a few exceptions to this such as the green of the Rifle Corps and the clothing of some of the regiments in the late 17th Century.

Before 1740 there are few surviving official records of the dress worn by the British Army, and although there are a certain amount of contemporary written descriptions available there are only a few drawings and paintings from which the early infantry dress can be reconstructed.

In 1660 The King's Royal Regiment of Guards (Grenadier Guards) are shown with the musketeers wearing an all red uniform, with a buff coat worn over the jacket (Fig 2)*. The officer at this period is shown wearing a blue coat laced with gold (Fig 1). This garment may be a civilian coat or a form of undress coat, since it is known that at this period officers in

*Throughout this book, figure references in parentheses indicate the appropriate uniform drawings in colour on pages 17, 21, 24, 25, 29, and 32. The key to each plate gives the contemporary title of the regiment concerned, with the 1914 title (if different) in parentheses.

1660-1670: *The infantry was composed of pikemen and musketeers. The first two figures in this group show the style of dress for musketeers, the loose buff coat being worn over the coloured uniform jacket. The musket was a matchlock, the pikemen having a full coat and a breastplate. The pike was about 16 feet in length. The end figure depicts an officer wearing the clothing worn in hot climate stations.* Colours: *Musketeers of Coldstream Guards, red with green cuffs, buff jacket, white bows. Pikeman of Coldstream Guards, green coat, red cuffs, breeches and stockings, white sash and bows. Officer of Coldstream Guards, 1670, all light grey with sky blue ribbons on hat, shoulder, knees and shoes. Baldrick (sword belt) was sky blue with gold embroidery.*

6

1660-1686: *The first figure is of an infantry officer, and the second a private, still armed with a matchlock and having the bandolier of cartridges. A typical dress of the period would be for the 9th Regiment, red lined orange, with white stockings and grey breeches. For the 2nd Regiment it would be red lined green, with green breeches and white stockings. The third figure is an officer of the Grenadier Company, Grenadier Guards. The coat is of a crimson colour with medium blue cuffs. The cap, belt and pouches were also medium blue with all lace and embroidery gold. The cravat was white, edged with a gold fringe. The fourth figure shows a Grenadier officer of the 11th Foot, 1686. The cap was light brown with a red bag, and the coat was red with light brown cuffs. Shoulder wings and braid were all edged with silver. The breeches and stockings were light brown, and the sash was crimson with silk fringes, gloves and belts were dark brown. The light brown is the same shade as the colour often referred to as gosling green.*

some of the European armies did not wear regulation uniform.

At this period the Coldstream Guards are shown as having green facings, the pikemen wearing a green coat with red cuffs. The coat reached to the knees, and was worn with red breeches and stockings and a white sash with green fringes. The figures depicting a grenadier and musketeer of the Coldstream Guards 1670 (Figs 3 and 4) show the loose fitting coats of the period and also the beginning of the special head-dress associated with the grenadier companies. This head-dress gradually became taller and more ornamental, and developed into the mitre cap.

The difference between the grenadier and the ordinary soldier can be seen in Figs 5 and 6. These represent a grenadier and musketeer of the regiment raised by John Granville, Earl of Bath, in 1685; this regiment became the 10th Foot and in 1881 received the title of The Lincolnshire Regiment. The significance of the status of a grenadier can be seen in the elaborate braiding on the coat, and this difference can again be seen in Figs 7, 8, and 9. These three figures show the clothing worn by a regiment raised in 1685 as 'Our Ordnance Regiment' (now the Royal Fusiliers). As there was no regular artillery at this time, King James II decided that an Ordnance Regiment should be raised for the care and protection of the cannon, which were kept at the Tower of London. As part of the Ordnance Regiment's duties was to protect the cannon when on the march, each man was armed with a fusil—a superior type of light musket. Since it was the first regiment to be fully armed with fusils, the King granted permission for the regiment to be styled 'Our Royal Regiment of Fusiliers'. The other arms carried were a bayonet and sword. Fig 10 shows the style of uniform worn by officers at this period, again a loose fitting coat, a waist sash and a baldrick over the right shoulder carrying the sword. Fig 11 shows the dress worn by a private of the Grenadier Guards in 1705.

From Fig 12 onwards we come to the period when there is a good amount of reference material to work from. In 1742 an official publication titled *A Representation of the Cloathing of His Majesty's House-*

1680-1732: *The left hand figure is a grenadier of 1680; the grenadier companies were added to infantry regiments in about 1678. The next figure is a Grenadier Guardsman of 1705. The hat was black with a white border and the coat red with blue collar and cuffs. All lace was white and belts were brown. They had brass buckles and the breeches were blue with white stockings. The third figure shows a grenadier of the Queen's (2nd Foot) in 1715. The cap was red with the Prince of Wales's crest. The small flap was blue with a white lamb. He wore a red coat with blue lapels and cuffs all decorated with the regimental pattern lace. Stockings were white and the belts and pouch were brown. The right hand figure is an officer of the 33rd Regiment in 1732. His dress was all red with silver lace, a crimson sash, white stockings, and a black hat edged with silver braid.*

1710-1735: *On the left is a grenadier of the 3rd Foot (Buffs) in 1725. He has an all buff cap with a black gryphon as a badge. Below this is a black grenade with red flames. The coat was red, the cuffs buff, the lace and gaiters white, and the belts brown. The figures shown next are an officer and private of the 1710 period. Typical dress would be red coats with yellow facings and silver lace for the officers, the sash being crimson with a silver fringe. The last man is a grenadier of the 1st Foot Guards (Grenadier Guards) in 1735, and he has a blue cap bearing the Crown and Garter Star. Below this a red flap with the White Horse of Hannover and the motto 'Nec Aspera Terrent'. The coat was red with blue lapels and cuffs, the lace being white. He wore buff belts and a 'GR' cypher in brass on the black pouch. The gaiters were white.*

hold and all the Forces upon the Establishment of Great Britain and *Ireland,* was prepared. This hand coloured work shows the uniforms worn by all the cavalry and infantry regiments. Fig 18 is based on the figure shown in this book. Line infantry regiments 1 to 50 are shown, all with full lapels except for numbers 18, 20, 38, 47, and the Invalids. Regiments 4, 7, 8, and 18, 21, and 23 have blue breeches, and the rest red except for the 42nd, a kilted Scots regiment. The facings are shown as:

| Colour | Regiment |
|---|---|
| Blue | 1, 4, 7, 8, 18, 21, 23, and Invalids |
| Deep Green | 2 and 46 |
| Green | 19 and 36 |
| Gosling Green | 5 |
| Medium Green | 11 |
| Olive Green | 24 |
| Pale Green | 39, 41 and 43 |
| Pale Buff | 14 and 22 |
| Buff | 3, 27, 31, 40, 42, and 49 |
| Yellow | 6, 15, 20, 25, 26, 28, 30, 34, 37, 38, 45, and 47 |

| Colour | Regiment |
|---|---|
| Deep Yellow | 9 and 13 |
| Bright Yellow | 10 |
| Light Yellow | 12 and 16 |
| Pale Yellow | 29 |
| Greyish White | 17 |
| Red | 33 |
| Orange | 35 |
| Black | 50 |
| White | 32, 44, 48 |

All regiments wore lace of regimental pattern. The waistcoats were red for all regiments except the following: 5th—Gosling Green, 20th—Yellow, 30th—Yellow, 35th—Orange, 39th—Pale Green. The pouch flap was light buff as were the belts, except for regiments 3, 4, 8, 11, 12, 13, 16,

1742-1751: *At this period the grenadiers and fusiliers wore the mitre cap, the battalion men being referred to as 'hat men'. The first figure is a Royal Welsh Fusilier of 1742. The coat was red with blue lapels, cuffs and turnbacks. All lace was of regimental pattern, in this case white with one edge of yellow and a tooth-shaped red line between the white and yellow. The waistcoat was red, the breeches blue, the gaiters white, the belts buff, and the pouch black. The Field Officer of 1745 shows the style of dress worn by infantry officers. Although the third figure is of the same period as the fusilier the coat is different to most of the 1742 regiments. Instead of the full lapels only white lace was worn on this coat. The regiment shown is the 20th Foot, the uniform being a red coat with yellow cuffs and turnbacks, a yellow waistcoat, red breeches and white gaiters. The right hand figure shows the dress worn by the Invalids in 1751; these Invalid Battalions were used for garrison duties, and were the predecessors of the Welch Regiment (41st Foot). Dress: red coat, blue cuffs and turnbacks, breeches and waistcoat and white gaiters.*

1751-1758: *The two infantry soldiers shown are wearing the marching order equipment. Although the coat is shown open it was usual to button the lapels over so that the front of the coat was closed. Besides the usual equipment a water canteen, haversack and a skin covered holdall were carried. The side arms were the 'Brown Bess' musket, a sword and a bayonet. The other figures show an officer and private on service in North America. The campaign dress at first was the same as for the first two figures but due to service conditions and lack of supplies many changes were made so that the appearance of the uniform altered considerably. The head-dress was altered by cutting the edges, the tails of the coat were cut off and officers dressed more in the fashion of the men. The tomahawk was used by the British Infantry and was carried in place of the sword.*

23, 24, 29, 38, 40, 41, 43, 44, 46, 47, 48, 49, and 50, with black flaps.

The style of dress worn by the Foot Guards in 1742 is shown in Figures 12 to 16. The officer carries a spontoon and the sergeant a halberd. The spontoon was discarded in 1786 and the halberd was gradually replaced after 1792. Sergeants then carried a pike. The drummer and fifer are wearing the Royal livery of red, blue and gold. Fig 16 is a grenadier company man. In the Guards at this time only the grenadier company wore the mitre caps, all battalion companies wearing the three cornered hat. Infantry officers of 1742 are given in Figures 17 and 23. Both officers are wearing a gorget; this is the small curved plate worn below the throat.

The dress of 1751 had a totally different appearance to the previous dress. The coat was now worn open and showed more of the waistcoat, but it was still buttoned across in marching order. The battalion companies still wore the three cornered hat and the grenadier companies the mitre cap. These latter were embroidered mostly in the same manner with a crown and Royal cypher, on a background of facing cloth with the red flap below having the White Horse of Hannover and the Motto 'Nec Aspera Terrent'. Certain regiments had a special device in place of the Crown and Cypher, amongst these the regiment which became the

1768-1777: *The sergeant carrying the halberd is from the 35th Foot 1777. Coat was red faced with orange on collar, cuffs and lapels. He wore white turnbacks, waistcoat and breeches, and a crimson sash with a central stripe of orange. The Light Company man of 1770 shown next is wearing the 1751 coat with the tails cut away. The head-dress is of leather. He is armed with a tomahawk as were other units serving in North America. The head-dress of the next soldier is black fur with gilt Crown and Cypher on the front, representing a private of the 11th Foot in 1770. The coat is red with collar, cuffs and narrow lapels of dark green. The turnbacks were white, as were the breeches and waistcoat. He wore black gaiters. The lace on the coat was white with two red and two green stripes. The end figure is that of an officer of the Grenadier Guards, 1776. He wore a black hat edged in gold, and a red coat with blue collar, cuffs and lapels, all laced in gold. He had white lining to his coat, white waistcoat, breeches and gaiters and crimson waist sash.*

Buffs had a Dragon, the Northumberland Fusiliers had St George and the Dragon, and the Royal Irish Regiment (Fig 19) the Irish Harp. Some regiments had wings on the coats as in Figs 19 and 22, while the other regiments were as in Figs 20 and 21.

Fig 24 shows the very elegant dress worn by an officer of a Royal regiment, in this case the Royal Fusiliers of 1756. The red, blue and gold of the coat shows well against the white waistcoat. Also the change in the cuffs from the previous period can be seen on the coat.

The four figures for 1768 depict (Fig 25) the 50th Foot; a regiment raised in 1755 (Royal West Kent Regiment); (Fig 26) the 53rd Foot (King's Shropshire Light Infantry); (Fig 27) the 66th Regiment of Foot (after 1881, the 2nd Battalion, Royal Berkshire Regt), and (Fig 28) a regiment raised in 1756 as the 2nd Battalion, 12th Foot, and renumbered 65th Regiment of Foot in 1758, becoming the York and Lancaster Regiment in 1881. The interesting points about these figures are the fur caps introduced shortly before 1768 and the white breeches, which were, however, replaced with buff for regiments with buff facings; the black

*FAR RIGHT: The 33rd Foot, 1799 (The Duke of Wellington's Rgt) was from 1782 to 1853 known as the 1st Yorkshire West Riding Regiment. The uniform shown is a scarlet coat with collar and cuffs of the same colour. The lace and buttons are silver, with the sash crimson, and gilt gorget. There is silver plate on the sword belt. The plume on the hat is red and white. In 1799 the 41st and 53rd Foot also had red facings. RIGHT: An officer of the 56th Regiment of Foot in 1800. He wears a black hat with red and white plume, a scarlet coat with purple facings and silver lace and buttons. In 1881 the 56th were amalgamated with the 44th Foot to form the Essex Regiment. The facings of the 56th were purple before 1881, being then changed to white. In 1936 the Essex Regiment was granted purple facings.*

gaiters were introduced in 1767 for line infantry, and on the coat the cuffs were made smaller. These figures have been based on a Manuscript Book in the Prince Consort's Library, Aldershot. A basic figure shows the regiments all with the same head-dress and the same shape of coat, the only difference being that some regiments have loops of square-ended lace whilst others are shown with bastion-shaped loops. This Manuscript Book can only be accepted as a rough guide to the period, as with most of these early works on uniforms. Many of the regiments shown were serving abroad and it was often many years before they caught up with the regulations.

The last type of long skirted open front coat worn by the infantry is given in Figures 29 to 40. Figs 29 to 34 illustrate the uniforms worn by the Coldstream Guards in 1790. Basically the three regiments of Foot Guards wore the same uniform except for the spacing of the buttons and lace, and certain small regimental distinctions. The Coldstream Guards shown wore their buttons and lace in pairs, the Grenadier Guards evenly spaced, and the Scots Guards in three's, a

1775-1804: *The first figure of this group shows the dress worn by all British Infantry in North America during the winter of 1775. It included a fur head-dress ornamented in some cases with a raccoon tail. The coat was made of white blanket material and had a band of light blue on the cuffs and another band around the bottom of the garment. The ties were light blue. Mittens were worn, and the gaiters were black. Next is shown a sergeant of the Battalion Company of the Grenadier Guards, 1790. He wore a black hat, with white feather tipped black. The red coat had blue collar, cuffs and lapels all with gold lace. There was a gold epaulette on the right shoulder, and a blue, edged gold, strap on the left shoulder. He had white lining to his coat, white waistcoat and breeches, black gaiters, and a crimson sash. The third figure is an officer of the Light Company of the Guards who wears a red coat with white lace. The end figure is a Field Officer of the 16th Foot in 1804. The coat is red with yellow facings and silver lace, and he has blue trousers trimmed with black.*

distinction retained to this day. The drummer, Fig 30, had single spaced bastion loops for the Grenadier Guards, and lace in two's and three's for the Coldstream and Scots Guards. The drummer's lace for the first two regiments was white with a blue fleur-de-lys pattern, and for the Scots Guards black with a yellow fleur-de-lys. The grenadier and battalion companies were also dressed in similar fashion with the usual regimental differences. For the Line Infantry the pattern was a red coat with collar, lapels and cuff of facing colour, and white turnbacks. In the case of regiments with buff facings the turnbacks, waistcoat and breeches were all buff. The lace for officers was gold or silver and the other ranks had lace of regimental pattern.

*RIGHT: The signals section of the 2nd Bn, Gloucestershire Rgt in 1900 showing the equipment for visual signalling in the field at this period. The standard of efficiency required of a regimental signaller was very high as he had to be proficient with flags, lantern and heliograph.*

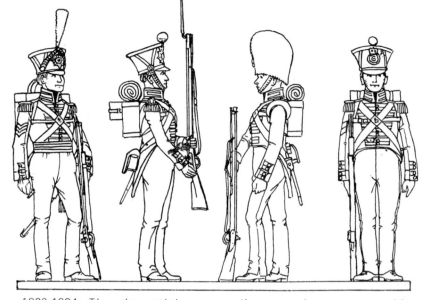

1832-1834: *The other ranks' pattern uniform was the red coatee with collar and cuffs of regimental facing colour, and white turnbacks. The coats were decorated with loops of white lace on the front, collar, cuffs and pocket flaps of the coat tails, white worsted epaulettes being worn by the battalion companies and wings by the grenadier and light companies. They wore dark trousers for winter and white for summer wear. The equipment consisted of a black pack and grey blanket worn on the back and a black ammunition pouch worn from a belt suspended over the left shoulder. All straps were white. The figures shown are from left to right, a sergeant of the 2nd Foot, 1832, a private of 1834, a private of the grenadier company, 6th Foot in 1844 and a corporal of the 16th Foot, 1844.*

was authorised in 1833, but the pocket flaps on the coatee were not worn after 1848 and the white trousers were replaced by grey in 1846. Among other changes of this period was the replacement of the bearskin cap of the grenadier companies by a shako in 1842, while the sergeants' sashes were changed to plain crimson in 1845.

Figures 59, 60, and 61 show the Light Infantry dress of 1839. The sergeant now had a coatee with no lace on the front, this new dress for sergeants being introduced in 1836.

The Grenadier Guards of 1832, Figures 62, 63, and 64, wear the bearskin cap granted to the regiment in July 1815 as a distinction for defeating the Grenadiers of the Garde Imperiale at Waterloo. The coat had a red collar for officers from 1831 to 1834 after which it was changed to blue, the collar and cuffs both having gold lace. Officers had a wide red band on the trousers but at this period the other ranks' grey trousers did not have a stripe. The sergeants had gold lace as usually worn by sergeants of Guards regiments.

The uniforms of the 1830s were perhaps the most elaborate and colourful that the British infantry had worn, but they were also the most

**Key to figures**

(107) 1914, The King's Royal Rifle Corps, Sergeant. (108) 1914, The King's Royal Rifle Corps, Rifleman. (109) 1914, The King's (Shropshire Light Infantry), Officer. (110) 1914, The King's (Shropshire Light Infantry), Sergeant. (111) 1914, The King's (Shropshire Light Infantry), Private. (112) 1914, The Gordon Highlanders, Officer. (113) 1914, The Gordon Highlanders, Sergeant. (114) 1914, The Gordon Highlanders, Private.

Officer's tunic, 1880 to 1914. Scarlet with collar and cuffs of facing colour, gold laced collar and cuffs, the collar and front edged white and a white stripe down skirt division at back, also on back of skirt a flap with white piping and 3 gilt buttons. Eight buttons on front. From 1880 to 1902 the ranks were shown by the lace on the cuffs and collar and by insignia on the shoulder cords. The tunic shown is for a Lieutenant Colonel, the Major has the same collar but with cuffs as shown next to tunic, next to this is the cuff for a Captain and above this cuffs for Lieutenants. Officers with rank below that of Major did not have the row of twisted cord on the collar. From 1902 the sash was worn round the waist and all officers had the same lace as shown for a Lieutenant on the cuffs and the collar without the row of twisted cords. Top centre is the gold braid shoulder cord.

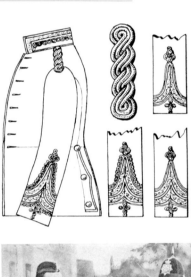

The Border Regiment, 1896; a sergeant in walking out dress and a private in full dress. The sergeant is wearing a glengarry. This Scottish head-dress was introduced to all infantry regiments in 1874. The familiar three chevrons as a badge of rank for sergeants was authorised by a General Order of 1802. Collar badges for infantry were introduced in 1876. The private has the Martini-Henry rifle and wears his marksman's badge on the left cuff. Note that for 'Guard Order', shown here, only one cartridge pouch and the bayonet frog were worn, not the full equipment.

32

Indian Mutiny and Crimea: *The first three figures illustrate infantry during the Indian Mutiny. When campaigning many combinations of dress were worn and these figures are based on contemporary drawings. The undress cap was worn, covered with a cloth and having a curtain protecting the neck. Soldiers fought at times in the grey shirt and blue trousers, or in the white or light drill uniforms. The officer is wearing the red shell jacket. The last figure is that of a private of infantry wearing trench order equipment during the Crimean War.*

*An officer wearing the uniform according to Dress Regulations, 1857. This consisted of a scarlet tunic with collar and cuffs of facing colour, gold lace, and badge of rank placed on collar. This officer may be an adjutant as the regulations give a brass scabbard for Field Officers, steel for Adjutants and black leather with gilt mountings for other officers. A detail drawing of the pattern of tunic worn by this officer is given on the next page.*

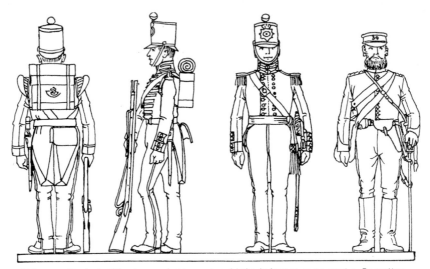

Crimean Period: *The two privates are a Light Infantry man and a Battalion man. The equipment consisted of a black knapsack worn on the back and a black ammunition pouch, all belts being white. Both men are wearing the Albert shako. The coatee shown was the last type to be worn by the British infantry. When the Crimean War started it was soon seen that this type of dress was most unsuitable for warfare and a new uniform was introduced featuring the double breasted tunic. The officer is shown in the last full dress coatee. This garment had collar and cuffs in facing colour, the fronts of the collar and the cuffs slashes being heavily ornamented with gold lace. The skirt turnbacks were white and the sash crimson. The last figure is of an officer in trench kit. The red shell jacket had collar and cuffs of facing colour, and the trousers, of dark Oxford mixture, almost black, were tucked into gum boots. During this campaign officers wore many odd forms of dress including civilian type jackets on occasions.*

*Officer's tunic, 1855 to 1874. This was of scarlet cloth with collar and cuffs of facing colour. It had gold lace, white piping, and gilt buttons. The badges of officers rank were worn on the collar. Field Officers had collars edged all round with gold lace. Captains, Lieutenants and Ensigns had gold lace on the top and front edges only. The collars shown are, from top to bottom, Colonel, Lieutenant Colonel, Major, Captain, Lieutenant, Ensign. For Field Officers the cuff had two rows of lace and the inner edges of the cuff slash and and the inner edge of the skirt flap were lined with gold lace. In 1868 the cuffs changed to pointed style.*

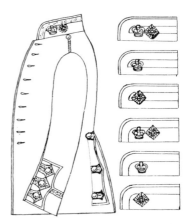

*Group of officers of the 51st Light Infantry, photographed at Curragh Camp on August 17, 1857. They are wearing the dark blue undress frock coat and crimson sashes. The 1857 Dress Regulations describe the Light Infantry forage cap as dark green with black silk oak leaf band and gold embroidered bugle above the number. The third officer from the left is from the 53rd Light Infantry, and wears the regimental number below the bugle. This was not done in the 51st. Note the waterproof leggings on the seated Major. An orderly stands on the far left.*

uncomfortable as can be seen in Figures 65 to 70; 65, 66, and 67 show the dress worn by a Line regiment, and 68, 69, 70 the dress of a Fusilier regiment, the main difference being the epaulettes for Line regiments, and the bearskin cap and wings for Fusiliers. The sergeant and private of Fusiliers are wearing a lace shape referred to as bastion. The officer, sergeant and private of the Rifle Brigade, Figures 71, 72, and 73, wear the shako with bronze appointments and the black ball tuft. The men's jackets were changed to double-breasted in 1833 and the white metal buttons were changed to black.

The last of the coatee uniforms, worn until the Crimean War, are shown in the three Royal Fusiliers figures Nos 74, 75, and 76. At this period came the change to the double-breasted full skirted tunic, with small turn-backed lapels in facing colour for officers. From this period the uniform gradually changed so that by 1895 the dress was almost the same as the last full dress of 1914. Only small detail alterations were made in the actual uniforms. For instance the other ranks' cuffs becoming pointed and the officers' cuffs had the elaborate braiding and lace indicating rank reduced to a single lace, edged with narrow braid.

The figures from 80 to 98 illustrate different branches of infantry during

*The officers of the 9th Foot (Norfolk Rgt) when stationed in India in 1878. The uniform worn is unusual in that the jacket is cut on the lines of a Norfolk jacket. The uniform was of a drab colour and in this photograph the glengarry is being worn. This was a universal undress headwear at this period. Four officers are wearing 'Poshteens'. These native coats, made of sheepskin with the hair inside the coat, were very popular on the North West Frontier stations.*

the last years of full dress uniform. When the Cardwell reforms of 1881 were introduced in the army, besides amalgamating units to make two battalion regiments it also meant that a new system of regimental facing colours was ordered. English and Welsh regiments were given white facings, Scottish yellow, and Irish green, while all Royal regiments retained their blue facings. By 1914 some regiments had received permission to revert to their old facing colour and these can be seen in the list of 1914 regiments which follows on page 37.

The regiments of Infantry were divided into Line, Fusiliers, Light Infantry, Highland and Lowland Scottish, and Rifles. The Scottish regiments are described in a separate book* and are not included here.

The dress of the Line regiments at 1914 consisted of the blue 'Universal Pattern' helmet, a scarlet tunic, and blue trousers with a narrow red stripe. The officer's tunic (Fig 104) had collar and cuffs of regimental facing colour. The cuffs were bordered at the top with gold lace, edged with a tracing cord and ending with a small Austrian knot at the top point. The buttons were equally spaced. On the back skirt were three buttons on each flap. On each shoulder was a triple plaited gold cord bearing the rank badges. For other ranks the tunic was as shown in Fig 105, the collar, cuffs and shoulder straps being of facing colour. The rank badges for all ranks below that of an officer were worn on the right arm only.

---

*SCOTTISH REGIMENTS, 1660-1914 (Almark Publications).

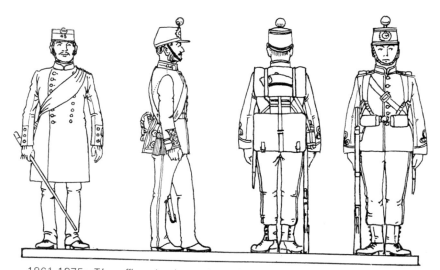

1861-1875: *The officer in the undress frock coat has a blue cap with a band of black braid round the lower section. In Royal regiments this band was red. The frock coat was dark blue with gilt buttons and the sash was crimson. The next officer is wearing the first pattern single breasted tunic which replaced the double breasted one of the Crimean War period. This was red with collar and cuffs of facing colour. The collar, cuffs and skirt flaps were ornamented with gold lace and all piping was white. The sash was crimson. The two privates are wearing the valise equipment, consisting of a black valise worn low on the back. The overcoat was carried across the shoulders. Between the valise and coat the mess tin was carried. The straps and pouches were white.*

## LINE REGIMENTS 1881 TO 1914

| Title | Pre-1881 title | Facings |
|---|---|---|
| The Queen's (Royal West Surrey Rgt) | 2nd Foot | Blue |
| The Buffs (East Kent Rgt) | 3rd Foot | Buff |
| The King's Own (Royal Lancaster Rgt) | 4th Foot | Blue |
| The Royal Warwickshire Regiment | 6th Foot | Blue |
| The King's Liverpool Regiment | 8th Foot | Blue |
| The Norfolk Regiment | 9th Foot | Yellow |
| The Lincolnshire Regiment | 10th Foot | White |
| The Devonshire Regiment | 11th Foot | Lincoln Green |
| The Suffolk Regiment | 12th Foot | Yellow |
| The Prince of Wales's Own (West Yorkshire Rgt) | 14th Foot | Buff |
| The East Yorkshire Regiment | 15th Foot | White |
| The Bedfordshire Regiment | 16th Foot | White |
| The Leicestershire Regiment | 17th Foot | White |
| The Royal Irish Regiment | 18th Foot | Blue |
| Alexandra, Princess of Wales's Own (Yorkshire Rgt) | 19th Foot | Grass Green |
| The Cheshire Regiment | 22nd Foot | Buff |

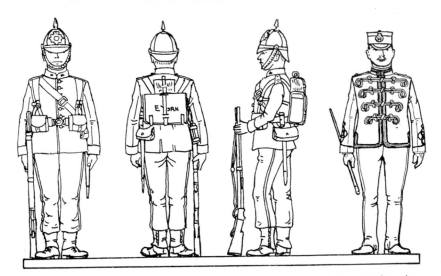

1878-1900: *The first three figures show the infantry private wearing the new 'Universal Pattern' helmet head-dress. The tunic was red with collar and cuffs in facing colour. The trousers were dark blue with a narrow red stripe and black gaiters and boots. The method of wearing the equipment had now changed and the valise was carried in the middle of the back with the mess tin on top of the valise. The haversack strap went over the right shoulder as previously worn. The water canteen was still on the right hip, and all straps and pouches were white with brass buckles. The fourth figure shows an officer wearing a patrol jacket. This was of universal pattern, in dark blue cloth with black braiding round the edges, black cords across the front, and with a black Austrian knot on each cuff. The trousers were dark blue with a narrow red stripe and the cap was dark blue with a black or red band and a regimental badge worn in front.*

| Title | Pre-1881 title | Facings |
|---|---|---|
| The South Wales Borderers | 24th Foot | Grass Green |
| The Gloucestershire Regiment | 28th & 61st Foot | White |
| The Worcestershire Regiment | 29th & 36th Foot | White |
| The East Lancashire Regiment | 30th & 59th Foot | White |
| The East Surrey Regiment | 31st & 70th Foot | White |
| The Duke of Wellington's (West Riding Rgt) | 33rd & 76th Foot | Scarlet |
| The Border Regiment | 34th & 55th Foot | Yellow |
| The Royal Sussex Regiment | 35th & 107th Foot | Blue |
| The Hampshire Regiment | 37th & 67th Foot | Yellow |
| The South Staffordshire Rgt | 38th & 80th Foot | White |
| The Dorsetshire Regiment | 39th & 54th Foot | Grass Green |
| The Prince of Wales's Volunteers (South Lancashire Rgt) | 40th & 82nd Foot | White |
| The Welsh Regiment | 41st & 69th Foot | White |
| The Essex Regiment | 44th & 56th Foot | White |

*Two sergeants and two privates of the East Yorkshire Regiment prior to the introduction of the Slade Wallace equipment, they are all wearing the old valise equipment of 1866 and are armed with the Lee-Metford Magazine rifle. Compare with drawings on page 38, but note the scarlet cloth protector worn on the shoulder.*

| Title | Pre-1881 title | Facings |
|---|---|---|
| The Sherwood Foresters (Nottinghamshire and Derbyshire Rgt) | 45th & 95th Foot | Lincoln Green |
| The Loyal North Lancashire Regiment | 47th & 81st Foot | White |
| The Northamptonshire Regiment | 48th & 58th Foot | White |
| Princess Charlotte of Wales's (Royal Berkshire Rgt) | 49th & 66th Foot | Blue |
| The Queen's Own (Royal West Kent Rgt) | 50th & 97th Foot | Blue |
| The Duke of Cambridge's Own (Middlesex Rgt) | 57th & 77th Foot | Lemon Yellow |

*Sergeant Major, Lance Corporal, Private, Colour Sergeant and Drummer of the York and Lancaster Regiment in 1890. Full dress, marching order and walking out dress are shown here. The regiment was an amalgamation in 1881 of the 65th and 84th Foot, the uniform is scarlet with white facings. Note the long service stripes worn on the cuff by ranks below sergeant, and the red sashes of the senior NCOs.*

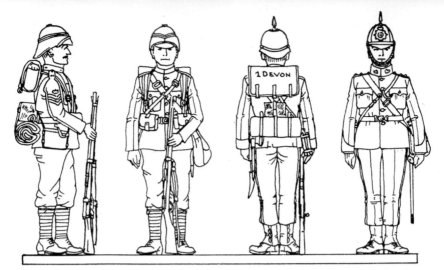

1900: *The two figures on the left give the campaign dress worn by the Northumberland Fusiliers at the start of the South African War. The helmet, uniform and puttees were all of a light khaki colour but the top folds of the helmet pugaree were red. On the jacket the buttons and shoulder titles were brass, and the rank stripes were of worsted lace. In this order of dress the Colour Sergeant at left wears a crown above three chevrons in place of the Colour badge. The Slade Wallace equipment carried featured a black valise at the shoulders with, at the waist, the rolled greatcoat and the mess tin in a waterproof cover above it. A water canteen and haversack were worn at the hips. The straps and ammunition pouches were white with brass buckles. The third and fourth figures show a private and officer in marching order. The private wears the blue helmet and a red tunic with collar and cuffs of facing colour. The Slade Wallace equipment is as before. The officer is wearing the red serge jacket with collar and cuffs of facing colour, breast pockets, and gilt buttons.*

| Title | Pre-1881 title | Facings |
|---|---|---|
| The Duke of Edinburgh's (Wiltshire Regt) | 62nd & 99th Foot | Buff |
| The Manchester Regiment | 63rd & 96th Foot | White |
| The Prince of Wales's<br>(North Staffordshire Rgt) | 64th & 98th Foot | White |
| The York and Lancaster Regiment | 65th & 84th Foot | White |
| The Connaught Rangers | 88th & 94th Foot | Green |
| The Prince of Wales's Leinster Regiment<br>(Royal Canadians) | 100th & 109th Foot | Blue |

## LIGHT INFANTRY REGIMENTS

The uniform of the Light Infantry was the same as for the Line Infantry regiments the only difference being in the helmet. For Light Infantry this was covered in dark green cloth. (Figs 109, 110, 111).

| Title | Pre-1881 title | Facings |
|---|---|---|
| Prince Albert's (Somerset Light Infantry) | 13th Foot | Blue |
| The Duke of Cornwall's Light Infantry | 32nd & 46th Foot | White |
| The Oxfordshire and Buckinghamshire<br>Light Infantry | 43rd & 52nd Foot | White |

| Title | Pre-1881 title | Facings |
| --- | --- | --- |
| The King's Own (Yorkshire Light Infantry) | 51st & 105th Foot | Blue |
| The King's (Shropshire Light Infantry) | 53rd & 85th Foot | Blue |
| The Durham Light Infantry | 68th & 106th Foot | Dark Green |

A special distinction of the Oxfordshire and Buckinghamshire Light Infantry was that officers did not wear collar badges; in place of these they wore gorget buttons and cords.

## FUSILIER REGIMENTS

Fusilier regiments wore a uniform the same as for Line Infantry except that officers wore a head-dress made of either black bear skin or black racoon skin, in appearance almost identical to the bearskin of the Brigade of Guards. For other ranks the head-dress was much smaller, and in the front was a grenade badge.

The plumes for the regiments were:

| | | |
| --- | --- | --- |
| The Northumberland Fusiliers: | on left, | bottom half white, top red. |
| The Royal Fusiliers: | on right, | white. |
| The Lancashire Fusiliers: | on left, | primrose yellow. |
| The Royal Welsh Fusiliers | on left, | white. |
| The Royal Inniskilling Fusiliers: | on left, | grey. |
| Royal Irish Fusiliers: | on left, | green. |
| The Royal Munster Fusiliers: | on right, | green base, white top. |
| The Royal Dublin Fusiliers: | on left, | green base, blue top. |

*LEFT: A Corporal and Private of The Buffs in 1895 wearing the full dress tunic.*

*BELOW: Rifle Regiments' jacket of Rifle Green cloth, with black braids and cords and collar and cuffs of facing colour. From 1902 the jacket was the same for all officers, but before this, rank was denoted by the collar and cuff embroidery as well as by the shoulder cords. Central lower figure is the cuff for a Captain, and next the cuff for a Field Officer of the KRRC. Above this is the cuff for a Field Officer of the Royal Irish Rifles and the Rifle Brigade.*

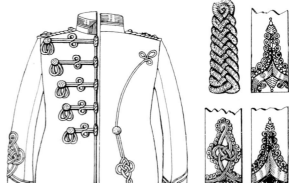

## FUSILIER REGIMENTS IN 1914

| Title | Pre-1881 title | Facings |
|---|---|---|
| The Northumberland Fusiliers | 5th Foot | Gosling Green |
| The Royal Fusiliers (City of London Regiment) | 7th Foot | Blue |
| The Lancashire Fusiliers | 20th Foot | White |
| The Royal Welch Fusiliers | 23rd Foot | Blue |
| The Royal Inniskilling Fusiliers | 27th & 108th Foot | Blue |
| Princess Victoria's (Royal Irish Fusiliers) | 87th & 89th Foot | Blue |
| The Royal Munster Fusiliers | 101st & 104th Foot | Blue |
| The Royal Dublin Fusiliers | 102nd & 103rd Foot | Blue |

## RIFLE REGIMENTS

The distinctive dress of the Rifle Regiments, although so dark was in fact a very attractive uniform. The busby was made from black Persian lamb, with black cords suspended across the front. The plumes were scarlet and black for The King's Royal Rifle Corps, black over green for The Royal Irish Rifles and black for The Rifle Brigade. The tunics were rifle green for all regiments, with scarlet facings for The King's Royal Rifle Corps, green for The Royal Irish and black for The Rifle Brigade. The officers' tunics were braided in Hussar fashion with five loops of black braid across the breast, and a black Austrian knot on each cuff. All wore black trousers, black buttons and equipment.

## GUARDS REGIMENTS

The Brigade of Guards are shown in Figures 98, 99, and 100. In 1914 there were four regiments of Foot Guards, namely the Grenadier Guards, raised in 1660, the Coldstream Guards, raised in 1650 as Colonel Monck's Regiment of Foot, the Scots Guards, a regiment revived in 1661, and the Irish Guards raised in April, 1900. The basic uniform for all regiments was the same, the distinctions for all regiments being in the bearskin cap plumes and the spacing of the buttons. For the Grenadier Guards the plume worn on the left was white and this plume was brushed into the bearskin so that it did not show from the front. The buttons were equal spaced. For the Coldstream Guards the plume worn on the right was red, the buttons being in pairs; on the front of the tunic from the collar down the buttons were arranged 2-2-2-2-1. The last button of the lowest pair was a flat button worn under the sash or belt buckle. The Scots Guards had no plume, on the front of the tunic the buttons were arranged 3-3-2. As in the Coldstream Guards the bottom button was a flat button worn under the sash or buckle. The buttons on the cuffs and tunic skirts were worn in threes. For the Irish Guards the plume worn on the right was of St Patrick's blue, and the buttons were spaced in fours. These uniforms substantially unaltered, are still worn by these regiments at the present time.

*RIGHT: A Quarter Guard of the Duke of Cornwall's Light Infantry in 1897. The way in which the Slade Wallace equipment was worn can be seen quite plainly in this picture. The regimental facings were white. Note the scarlet cloth protector on the left shoulder to reduce wear on the tunic with rifles at the slope.*

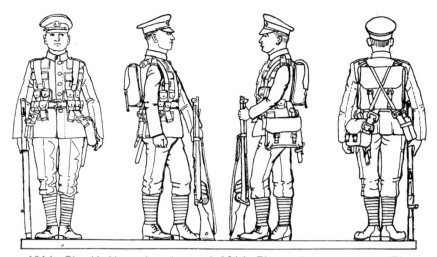

*1914: The khaki service dress of 1914. The equipment worn is 'The Pattern 1908 Web Infantry Equipment'. The men are in marching order. The equipment was made up of a waistbelt, a bayonet frog, 2 braces, cartridge carriers, pack, haversack and water bottle. The haversack was worn at the left hip, the water bottle on the right. An entrenching tool carrier could be worn with this equipment, the head behind the water bottle and the handle fixed to the bayonet frog. In fighting order only cartridge carriers, bayonet, entrenching tool, water bottle and haversack were carried, the latter on the back in place of the pack. The water bottle was then strapped on behind the haversack. All buckles were brass and self locking. Boots were black for other ranks, but officers and Sergeant Majors had brown boots.*

## APPENDIX 1: SOME INFANTRY WEAPONS

*Key to illustrations on next two pages:*

(1) Musketeer's Bandolier, 1660. (2) Matchlock Musket, 1660 to 1700. (3) Flintlock Musket, 1700, with dog safety catch. (4) Flintlock Musket of 1714 with dog safety catch. (5) Flintlock Musket 1750 to 1840. The 'Brown Bess'; various types similar to this were in use. (6) Plug Bayonet, 1680-1700. (7) Trowel Plug Bayonet, 1680. (8) Ring Plug Bayonet, 1690-1701. (9) A Matchlock. (10) A Flintlock. (11) The Baker Rifle and Sword Bayonet of 1800. (12) Officer's Sword 1660. (13) Officer's Sword, early 18th Century. (14) Officer's Sword, early 18th Century. (15) Officer's Sword, 1796. (16) Officer's Sword, 1786. (17) Officer's Court Sword, early Victorian. (18) Officer's Sword, 1822. (19) Officer's Sword, 1803. (20) Officer's Sword, 1895. (21) Sergeant's Pike, 1792-1830. (22) Sergeant's Halberd, 1700-1792. (23) Officer's Spontoon, 1700-1786. (24) The Brunswick Rifle, 1837; the first percussion rifle. (25) The Percussion Musket of 1842. (26) The Minie Rifle of 1851. (27) The Enfield Rifle, 1855. (28) The Short Enfield Rifle, 1860. (29) The Snider Rifle, 1865. (30) The Martini-Henry Rifle, 1871. (31) The Lee-Metford Rifle, 1888; the first magazine rifle. (32) The Lea-Enfield Rifle, 1895. (33) The Lee-Enfield Rifle, 1902.

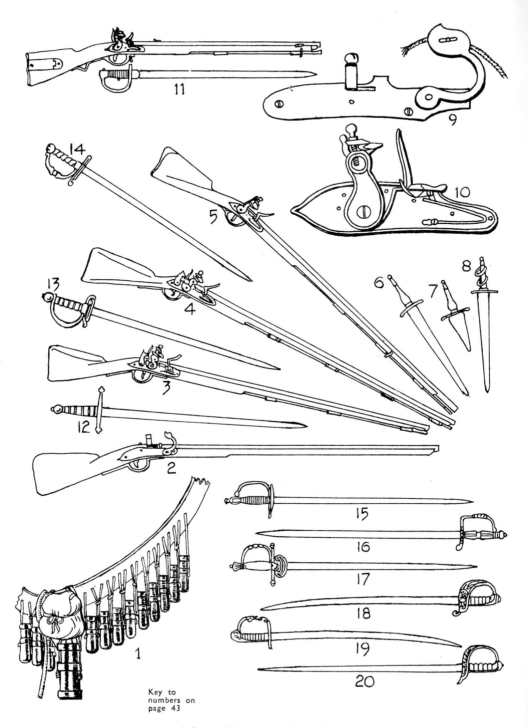

**Infantry Weapons, 1660-1914**

Key to numbers on page 43

44

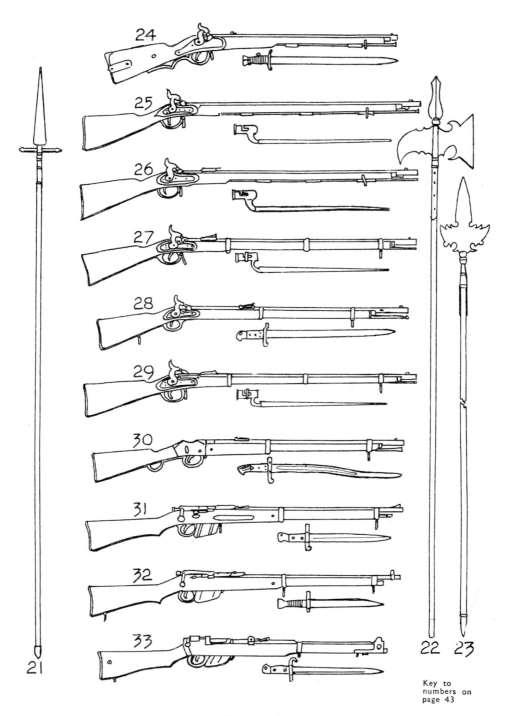

**Infantry Weapons, 1660-1914**

Key to numbers on page 43

## APPENDIX 2: INFANTRY HEAD-DRESS, 1800 to 1914

**The Stove Pipe Shako, 1800-1812. (Figures 1, 2 and 3):** The shako of 1800, 8 inches high, was made of black lacquered leather, changed to felt in 1806. The plate was gilt for officers and brass for other ranks. Above the plate was a black cockade with a button in the centre. The plumes were white for Grenadier Companies, dark green for Light Companies and white above red for Battalion Companies. Figure 3 shows the back peak worn on some issues of this shako. Figure 7, shows the shako worn by Light Infantry and Rifles, as usually depicted, black with a black rosette and green plume.

**The Waterloo Shako, 1812-1816. (Figures 4, 5 and 6):** Made of black felt, this head-dress was made with a false front which gave it a height of $8\frac{1}{4}$ inches. This front had a binding of black braid. The plate was gilt for officers and brass for other ranks. The officer's cap lines were gold and crimson, the other ranks white. Some Light Infantry companies wore dark green cords. For Light Infantry regiments the cords were dark green and on or below the cockade a small silver bugle was worn. Grenadier Companies had a small gilt grenade. The plumes were the same as for the previous shako. Early in 1815 the plate was discarded for Rifle and Light Infantry Corps and Companies in favour of a Bugle Horn with Strings and the regimental number below the strings.

**The Regency Shako 1816-1829. (Figures 8 to 12):** Figures 8 and 9 show the officers' black felt shako with a black peak, about $7\frac{1}{2}$ inches high, slightly bell-topped. Around the top was a band of $2\frac{1}{2}$ inch wide gold or silver lace; around the base was a band $\frac{3}{4}$ inch wide. The plate was usually gilt, but sometimes silver, with either a number or regimental device. Above the round plate was a crown. Surrounding the plate was a circle of gold or silver lace with a central line of crimson. At the top on the band of lace was a black cockade. Above this was the plume, 12 inches high. The plumes were white for Grenadier Companies, green for Light Companies and white over red for Battalion Companies. The chin scales were gilt or silver according to the regimental lace and buttons. Figure 10 shows the alterations to the officers' shako in 1822. It was made 1 inch taller and with a silver star plate, the back peak being discontinued. It must be noted that the shako plates varied considerably and those shown are only a guide to the general style of the period. Figure 11 is the other ranks' shako worn from 1816 to 1829. The details are as for Figures 8 and 9 but of inferior quality. Light Infantry Regiments and Light Companies wore the Regency shako with a silver 'bugle and strings' badge and dark green cords as in Figure 12. Light Company men wore a white metal bugle as a badge.

**The Bell-Topped Shako 1829-1844. (Figures 13 to 16):** This was of black beaver. Figures 13 and 14 show the officers' shako of 1829 to 1835, the top and base were edged with black leather, as also were the V-shaped side straps. There was no lace or cockade on this head-dress. The badge was a gilt star with a crown. The central device was a silver star with regimental symbol. It had gilt chin scales. The plume worn from 1829-1830 was of swan feather. From 1830-1831, it was white over red 12 inches tall. From 1831-1835 it was white and 8 inches tall. The plume was replaced by a tuft in 1835, this being white for Line Regiments, dark green for Light Infantry and black for Rifles; see Figure 15. Figure 16 shows the other ranks' shako, 1829-1839, the plume being replaced by the ball tuft in 1835. Figures 17 and 18 give the alterations of 1839, the shako being slightly taller with a new type of badge.

**The Albert Shako, 1844-1855, (Figures 19 to 22):** This was made of black beaver with black leather bands at the top and base. The ball tufts for Line Infantry were white from 1844 to 1846, then red and white for Battalion Companies, and white for Grenadier Companies and Fusilier Regiments. From 1844 the Light Infantry Companies and Regiments still wore the green ball tuft and the Rifles wore black. A 'Universal Pattern' gilt star was worn, the star bearing the regimental distinctions. There was a gilt chin chain. Figure 21 is the shako for a Fusilier regiment. Figure 22 is the shako for line infantry, other ranks.

**The Shako of 1855 to 1861. (Figures 24, 25 and 26):** Made of black felt, $5\frac{1}{2}$ inches in front, $7\frac{1}{4}$ inches at back. Figure 24 is the other ranks' head-dress. Figures 25 and 26 show the officers'. The plate was of Universal Pattern but there were many regimental variations. The other ranks' shako had ventilators at the sides and the officers' had one at the back in the shape of a Gorgon's Head. Field Officers wore gold lace round the top, 2 rows for Colonels and Lieutenant Colonels, 1 row for Majors. The ball tuft remained the same as for the previous shako. In 1856 Light Infantry Regiments adopted a dark green drooping plume, and the Fusiliers a similar plume in white. Some Light Infantry regiments had the 'bugle and strings' badge. Fusiliers had a grenade badge.

**The Shako of 1861-1869. (Figure 27):** Made of blue cloth, 4 inches high at front and $6\frac{1}{4}$ inches at back. The cloth covering the shako was quilted, making this a rather unusual head-dress. Round the top there were 2 bands of gold lace for Colonels and Lieutenant Colonels and one band for Majors, the mens' shako was almost identical except that it was made of cheaper materials. The plate again was of 'Universal pattern' but with the usual regimental distinctions. The ball tuft was slightly smaller than that on the previous shako but the colours remained the same.

**The Shako of 1869 to 1878. (Figures 28 and 29):** This was the last pattern shako worn by the British Infantry. It was of dark blue cloth, with, for officers, two bands of gold braid round the top and a narrow band round the base, plus a band of gold braid from top to base each side and one at the back. The plate was different to previous ones being a garter with the regimental number or device in the centre, surrounded by a laurel wreath and surmounted by a crown. The ball tufts were the same as before. For Light Infantry regiments the shako was dark green with a dark green drooping hair plume.

**Figure 30** shows the Fusiliers cap introduced around 1866.

**Figure 31** is the busby worn by Rifle Regiments from 1871.

**Figure 32:** The 'Universal Pattern' helmet introduced in 1878, blue cloth for Line Infantry Regiments and dark green cloth for Light Infantry Regiments.

46

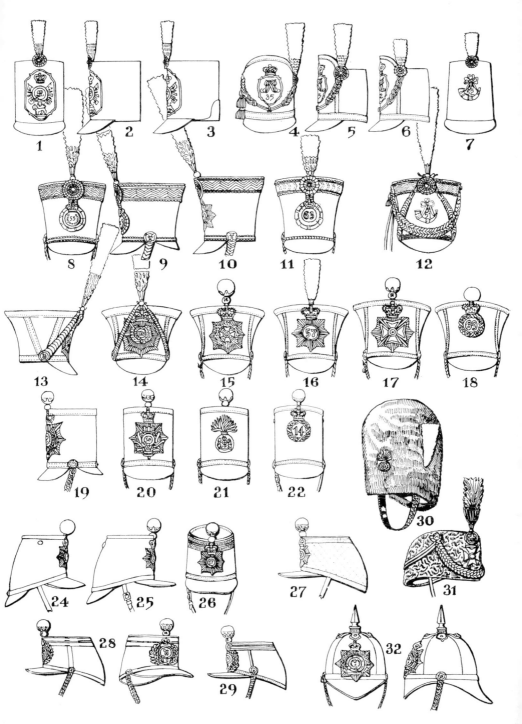

ABOVE, LEFT: Men of a line regiment changing guard, 1897. Wearing the full dress uniform, the sergeant can be seen to have the piece of scarlet cloth that was worn on the left shoulder to protect the tunic from being rubbed by the rifle. The back of the privates' tunic was changed in 1902 to a 3 pointed slash with 3 buttons on each side of the skirt. ABOVE, RIGHT: Three privates of the South Wales Borderers in 1895. The man on the left is in walking out dress and the central figure is a regimental orderly. Both are wearing the second tunic which was mostly used so that the dress tunic could be kept for parade. This is shown on the private in full marching order, his tunic having a white piping on the front edge. His rifle is the Magazine Lee-Metford and he is wearing the Slade Wallace equipment.

These soldiers of the Suffolk Regiment on overseas service, c. 1900, are wearing the light khaki drill uniform; the belt, pouch and haversack are part of the Slade Wallace equipment. The topi had a white puggaree with the regiment badge placed in the centre. This picture shows one of the methods of supplying water to troops away from base. Note the regimental name stencilled on the water bottles.